Soar 2 Success In Sales & Marketing

78 Tips to D.R.A.S.T.I.C. Results

10/28/16

Alicia,

Thank you for taking the drastic step and coming to Houston. You are certainly soaring to success!

Toni

By
Elizabeth
McCormick
And
Toni Harris

Published by Soar 2 Success Publishing

ISBN: 9781943043071

Printed in the United States of America

Book Design by Chris Mendoza
chrisdmendoza.com

Table of Contents

Dedication

This book is dedicated to our collaborators, joint venture partners, and supporters.

We couldn't do what we do without YOU!

A Note from Toni

Welcome to Soar 2 Success with Sales and Marketing – 78 Tips to get D.R.A.S.T.I.C. Results!

As a marketing strategist, I often see where business owners don't work enough on their business because they are too busy working in their business. In order for a business to not only survive, but also thrive marketing the business must be a constant. This book helps you to implement tips in your sales and marketing strategies to get increased results. It takes the sting out of sales and marketing and gets you one step closer to your goals.

Let us know what tips and tweaks you implemented and how they made a drastic change in your business. Happy sales & marketing!

Success happens when you take drastic steps!

Toni ☺

A Note from Elizabeth

Welcome to Soar 2 Success!

Your place for tips and tweaks to help you in your achievement.

Whether you are the owner of a business and in charge of sales or work in a sales department and need to close more sales, this book is for you.

Toni and I take you through Toni's DRASTIC framework, the 7 sections of tips to get you closer to the results you desire.

Be sure to visit the Soar2Success.com for more resources!

Are you ready to SOAR?

Elizabeth McCormick

Drastic Results

Tip #1

Baby Steps

Drastic steps aren't necessarily gigantic steps. Sometimes a drastic step is a baby step. Baby steps keep you moving forward. Don't think that your drastic steps have to be huge; small steps count too.

Every time you step outside of your comfort zone, it's a drastic step no matter how small.

Drastic Results Tip #2

Create a Roadmap

When you want drastic results, write down your goals.

Review them often. Create a "roadmap" to achieve your goals. Identify the people, places and things you need to achieve your goal as your resources.

Write them down and contact them, yes ASK, for help.

Identify the steps you want to take and keep steppin'!

Drastic Results
Tip #3

Keep Steppin'

Life happens, but so what!

Do you think successful people don't have obstacles in their way? Of course they do! It's the successful person who can keep moving over, around and through the obstacles.

In fact, many successful people look at life's challenges as stepping stones to their goals.

Life moves fast, don't let it slow you down or keep you from reaching your goals.

Drastic Results
Tip #4

Get Committed, Stay Committed

Commitment to your goals is key to achievement.

Without commitment, you will give up at the first obstacle. Anything worth having is worth renewing your commitment.

There may be times during your sales journey where you will want to quit, but stay committed to the outcome and refuse to let your obstacles win.

Remove the commitment stealers from your path so that you can keep on steppin' no matter what!

Drastic Results
Tip #5

Get Some Help

Asking for help is drastic!

It is sometimes easier to do the task yourself than to ask for help. Ask yourself:

Are you doing tasks that an administrative assistant should be doing?

Are those tasks a distraction from the hard part of making the sale?

If you find yourself spending more time shuffling papers than making sales, take the drastic step and get some help!

Drastic Results
Tip #6

Just Chill

Take a break. Breaks are necessary to rejuvenate.

Rejuvenating is important to help you to be successful. If you don't rest your brain and your body, they will stop you. Your body can shut down if you don't take the drastic step to chill out and relax.

When you step away from the work, it gives you a fresh perspective when you do go back to it.

Plus, your family needs you to slow down and give them time and attention. It doesn't do any good to achieve success and lose your family, so just chill.

Drastic Results
Tip #7

Show Up

Half the battle to success is showing up! But what does showing up mean?

Attending a networking event, going to the trade show, even when you don't feel like it; pushing through to your appointments. Being in the right place at the right time is what grows your business. It doesn't happen on your couch.

Connecting with a person who can buy or who can connect you to the resources you need to grow to the next level are priceless to your success.

So the next time you don't want to go, show up anyway!

Drastic Results

Tip #8

Say YES!

Is there a big goal you want to achieve?
What are the baby steps you have to take to achieve that goal?
What do you get to say yes to that helps
you to achieve that goal?

When taking drastic steps, it often takes
a simple yes to activate your action.

Say yes and figure out the how later.

In what areas can you say yes to yourself that gets you closer to your goal? Share your "YES" items with Toni and Elizabeth at:
Soar2Success.com/Say-Yes

Drastic Results
Tip #9

Do the Right Thing

Sometimes it takes a drastic step to do the right thing in sales. Salespeople get a bum wrap because of the few who utilize shady sales practices.

Sales is a noble and necessary profession that fuels our economy. Without salespeople and the sales they bring, there is no business, so be proud to sell!

When selling, always do the right thing for your clients and business will flow. Treat people the way you want to be treated in the sales process and it will show in your sales presentations.

Look out for your client and your business will flourish.

Drastic Results
Tip #10

By Any Means Necessary

Success doesn't happen by accident.
Success is very deliberate and intentional.
Obtaining knowledge, putting your head down
and grinding through action create success.

Success means getting up early and going to bed late.
Success means consistency.
Success means showing up even when you don't
feel like it and success means taking drastic steps
that may be out of your comfort zone.
Success isn't only about showing up, successful
people make it happen by any means necessary.

Are you ready for success?

Determine Your Niche

Tip #11

Nobody Serves Everybody

Narrowing your niche can be hard to do because you think you are missing out on business.

A niche creates a focal point for your sales and marketing efforts. Defining your niche can GROW your business!

Having a niche does not mean you can't serve other people, but narrowing your focus means you are clear who you are looking for as your ideal client.

Determine Your Niche

Tip #12

Who Do You Love?

A good way to define your target market is to take a look at who you love and who loves you.

For instance, when Toni was a financial advisor, it was a natural market for her to target working women and more specifically minority women. Toni has an understanding of who they are and what they need as women and mothers. She also could speak their language and serve them well when it came to educating them about investing.

So who is it that you can naturally serve? Once you answer that question, go after them and use your love for who they are to serve them well.

Determine Your Niche
Tip #13

Who Is Underserved?

Another way to define your niche is to examine who is underserved. Perhaps there is a target market that is overlooked because of demographics or socioeconomic status (this counts for the wealthy too). Many people take for granted that the wealthy are overserved, because they are simply wealthy; however, that may not necessarily be the case.

The consumers in the wealthy target market are busy. They are typically the Type A personalities that have their head down and don't have time to figure out how to get what you sell.

Don't be afraid to niche yourself in an area that may at first seem intimidating, you will likely find that they need you and they will refer you to their friends who have the same needs.

Determine Your Niche
Tip #14

Location, Location, Location!

Can you define your target market by location? Are you in an area where you can hone in on your location.

Consider a realtor that was an area specialist. She sold homes in other areas but when it came to her neighborhood she knew everything there was to know about it. She had signs all over the neighborhood, which is why it was easy to call her. She is an excellent example of how defining a niche works.

Are you the "go-to" person in your field? Are you known by your niche? If you are not, you should be.

Be the area specialist and business comes to you.

Determine Your Niche

Tip #15

Paint a Picture

Who is your current ideal client? What about them do you like? Do you like how they interact with you? Do you like how they take your advice? Do you like how they implement?

Whatever you like about your current client "paint a picture" of who they are and go after them. Let them know how much you appreciate them as a client and ask them for referrals to more people like them. Be sure you know how to describe them to other people too. That way you are sure to get more qualified prospects and not just names.

Brains are wired for specificity. So get really clear and specific about your ideal client.

Determine Your Niche

Tip #16

Introduce Yourself

What's your 30-second elevator pitch? Talk about the benefits of what you do, not the features. This is the time the audience will get to know YOU, focus on YOU and become aware of the impact you have on others!
Questions to answer in your commercial:
Start by asking a question to grab your listener's attention
Who is your ideal client, niche and what solutions you provide
END with your NAME so you are remembered!
You want listeners to recognize themselves in the description and basically raise their hand and say, "That's me!" or "I know someone."

Want some feedback? Video yours, save to you-tube and post the link at ***Soar2Succss.com/introductions***

Determine Your Niche

Tip #17

Be Referrable

Having a niche makes you more referrable.

It makes your networking friends know exactly whom they can refer to you. For instance, if you are a financial advisor and you are looking to get into companies, you could say something like, "I'm looking for Human Resource Directors or CFOs who are complaining about their current retirement plan."

You would listen for clues such as, "we don't have enough participation," or "the fees we pay are too much." This tells your referral network what to listen for as they are moving around in their sphere of influence.

Remember, the more specific you are- the better!

Determine Your Niche

Tip #18

Choose One, Then Another

Lots of people resist choosing a niche because they think they have to stay there forever!

Niches can be flexible. Once you develop your current niche or get bored with it, choose another one. You are not tied to your niche market forever.

Niche marketing is a tool to help you to find your target. Of course, you are going to hit outside the target sometimes and it doesn't mean you have to let that business go.

If you aim for the target you are more likely to hit the bulls eye!

Determine Your Niche

Tip #19

Become The Expert

The other benefit of a niche is that you become the expert.

Once word gets out that you are the go-to person that serves your target market, they will be all over you! You can speak in front of that market, you can network in that market, you can join online social media groups that target that market, you can write articles to magazines that target that market.

There is so much fun you can have in a niche without the stress of serving everyone, and be recognized as the expert while you are at it!

Determine Your Niche

Tip #20

Get Smart

Putting in the time and research to hone in on your niche is a smart decision. Identifying your target market keeps you from running to every networking event and conference. It saves you time, money, energy and frustration when deciding how to spend your marketing energy.

Identifying and marketing to your niche keeps you from getting overwhelmed by trying to become an expert in many industries.

Simply put, defining your target audience is SMART!

Relationships Turn Contacts to Contracts

Tip #21

Set a Goal

Relationship building starts with networking.

When networking, it is not the goal to meet everyone in the room. You should concentrate on connecting with a set number of people. 3-5 people is a great quality goal.

Once you meet 5 people that you wanted to connect to, the presssure is off and then you're essentially done with your networking. Keep in mind; You may meet a total of 20 people, but focusing on meeting your goal of 5 brings you a level of satisfaction.

Relationships Turn Contacts to Contracts

Tip #22

Ask for a One-on-One Appointment

When networking, ask your new acquaintance if they would be interested in getting together for coffee so that you can learn more about whom they are and what they do. You want to help them in their business.

Of course, they want to tell you more about them. Most people love talking about themselves!

Use that coffee time to begin to build a relationship to see how you can become a referral source for one another.

Relationships Turn Contacts to Contracts

Tip #23

Ask For a Date!

When your new acquaintance agrees to a one-on-one networking appointment, ask them right then for a date!

No, not the intimate kind of date but a date for the networking coffee chat. Most people have their calendars on their mobile device and can schedule a date on the spot. When they agree to have a coffee with you, say, "Great! Do you have your calendar with you?" If they do, pull out your device and schedule the coffee chat right there at the event. That way when you leave the event you leave with five appointments on your calendar. This eliminates the chance that "someday we will get together" will never come.

Relationships Turn Contacts to Contracts

Tip #24

Use a Checklist

When doing the one-on-one appointment, have a checklist to guide you through the appointment. This allows you to have a systematic way to get acquainted with the person and makes sure that you cover the basics when getting to know the person. The person who speaks first wins! So get control of the meeting by asking who they are and who is an ideal referral for them. Take your notes on the checklist and use it as a reference when you return to your office.

Download a Sample Networking Checklist:
Soar2Success.com/networking-checklist

Relationships Turn Contacts to Contracts

Tip #25

Give First!

If you know someone that can help them, be generous and give them a lead. Use texting, social media or email to complete an e-intro on the spot. This endears them to you and they will feel the need to do the same for you.

A relationship is built on a foundation of giving because you genuinely want to help someone, not because of what they can do for you.

However, if you make an impression on them because you are willing to help them out, then even if they don't have a lead for you, they will follow you and become a referral source in a different way.

Relationships Turn Contacts to Contracts

Tip #26

Fortune in the Follow-Up

Do you have a system for follow up after the event? As the saying goes, the fortune is in the follow up. If you don't have a fortune perhaps you are not following up.

Statistics say it takes 6-12 touches before a person will do business with you but most of us give up after 3 attempts. We take it personal and rationalize that the person is just not serious about connecting. Perhaps, no one has taught them the power of networking and that the real relationships are built after the event.

If it is someone you really want to connect with, don't give up! After all, the fortune truly is in the follow-up.

Relationships Turn Contacts to Contracts

Tip #27

It's Not About You!

When connecting with someone in a networking environment. Let them talk. Ask questions to get them talking about themselves. Ask them what they need? Who's their ideal client? How can you help them? Make the conversation about them.

In turn, they are likely to be as interested in you as you are in them. They will ask you the same questions and this is your time to answer them. They will walk away thinking, "Wow! This person really cares about me."

It's all because you made it about them.

Relationships Turn Contacts to Contracts

Tip #28

Online or Offline?

That is the current great debate! Many people prefer online networking because it's international and can grow your network exponentially. It also allows you to connect with people on a different level by engaging with them personally as well as professionally. There is a lot to love about online networking!

Try connecting offline first and then taking the relationship online. Nothing beats the eye-to-eye contact, shaking hands and giving hugs. There is something about the human touch.

So when you are able to choose, try offline first, then online.

Relationships Turn Contacts to Contracts

Tip #29

Take the online, offline

Some of the best relationships come from when you take the online relationship offline.

Why not have a "Facebook Friends Fellowship" and invite your online friends to meet in person? When you meet in person there's an instant connection. You may feel that you have known each other and it's just a matter of catching up.

When traveling to another city, reach out to your connections in that city in advance of your trip. Set up shop at a coffee house and invite your online friends to come meet you in person. You'll be surprised how many people will show up which allows the real connecting to begin.

Relationships Turn Contacts to Contracts

Tip #30

Get Involved

The deeper relationships come from when you get involved in networking groups or conference committees.

This is how you build relationships with key people in any organizations. They get to know you, you get to know them and deeper connections happen.

So when you can, get involved, share your gifts and the relationships will grow and so will your business.

Accountability Systems

Tip #31

Mentor Someone

The best way to learn is to teach.

Helping someone else in their business or job has great rewards. The first is that you gain fresh perspective in the process. Seeing their business as new can open your eyes to different possibilities of what could happen in your business.

The second benefit is when you help someone else; it boosts your confidence in your abilities and keeps you focused on the positive.

And the 3rd benefit? The person you are mentoring becomes your champion.

Accountability Systems

Tip #32

Hire a Coach

One of the best investments you can make in yourself is to hire a coach.

Early in her financial advising career, Toni hired a coach. She still operates by some of the principals she learned in that relationship. Although she was barely making money, she knew she needed to take a drastic step and get help. That year Toni made over $160,000.

You may not be able to see what is getting in your way. A coach will help you to see clearly. If you want to succeed, do like all the pro athletes do, hire a coach!

Accountability Systems
Tip #33

Give Accountability a Hug

Don't dread being held accountable, embrace it.

It is a good thing to have someone to be accountable to. Someone who can call out your stuff when you are not fully playing all out. When you are letting yourself off the hook, your accountability partner can give you the swift kick you need to play at the level you know you can.

So the next time you get annoyed because your coach called you on the carpet, pause, and thank them because the next time, you will get your commitments complete and you will give them a hug!

Accountability Systems

Tip #34

Write it Down!

An effective technique for being accountable is writing your thoughts down! When you get the task out of your head and put it on paper, you no longer rely on your memory.

By listing tasks out, more gets done and the feeling of productivity and accomplishment increases.

Also, be sure to write down due dates and by when you must have the task completed. This too will make sure that you stay accountable to yourself.

Prioritize these items by circling the most important items to accomplish and do those first.

Accountability Systems

Tip #35

Are You "NO" Challenged?

Is the reason you can't get your stuff done because you have a hard time saying, "No!"? Do you get bogged down doing stuff for your kids, your spouse, your boss, serving on too many committees, community projects, etc.

You will have to learn the power of no. No is a powerful word when you use it in a loving way. It is better for you to say no and get your own projects and work completed so that you can later have the time and space to serve those other people. Otherwise, your time is eaten up by other people's stuff and you are wondering why your stuff didn't get done. And remember, "NO" is a complete sentence, it does not require any explanation.

Accountability Systems
Tip #36

Take Personal Responsibility

It is great to have an accountability partner to check in with on your goals. However, it is most important to take personal responsibility and be accountable to yourself first and foremost.

Accountability to yourself is key to accomplishing your goals and even your daily to-do list. Personal responsibility says that you take ownership for the outcome, either way.

When you fail to deliver on a task, don't look to the shoulda, woulda, coulda, look at the situation and ask yourself, "what could I have done differently to change the outcome?"

Next time make a different choice for an entirely different outcome.

Accountability Systems

Tip #37

Put It On The Calendar

"What gets on your Calendar, gets done"
~Elizabeth McCormick

Schedule the things that are important to get done. If you have to complete a proposal, schedule it and set an alarm.

If something is important, don't let time get away from you. Use accountability systems such as Google calendar, OneNote, Evernote or some other tracking system to make sure you stay on track.

Be aware of your high performance times. When do you "feel" more productive and get more done? Those are not the times to have meetings or phone calls. Protect those times for the more difficult tasks you need to accomplish.

Accountability Systems

Tip #38

Communicate

Communicate with your boss what you are up to. That's a sure fire way to get you motivated to do the things that need to get done. Make sure you tell them when they can expect it to be done and ask them to check in with you on the progress.

Your boss wants you to succeed and most will be happy to know that you are relying on them to help you to get stuff done. I know it's drastic to tell the boss, but do you want to get it done or not? If so, tell the boss!

What if you ARE the boss? Communicate to your team or your coach your goals and ask them to hold you to them!

Speak to Influence
Tip #39

Speak for Sales

Speaking is one of the best marketing tools you can use to grow your business.

As a speaker in front of the room you are the "go-to" expert. Speaking allows you to build a one-to-many relationship in addition to a one-to-one relationship.

Whether you're presenting a project or idea in a small group setting, or in the front of large arena sharing a concept or keynote, there is an instant credibility from leading in the front of the room.

The instant credibility opens the doors to sales opportunity.

Speak to Influence

Tip #40

Develop a Signature Talk

What's a signature talk? A signature talk is one that motivates your audience to action because of the way you have structured your message.

When you can, incorporate a motivational message into your speech. Educate your audience and give them "a-ha" moments that make them think deeper and change their behavior.

Make your presentations interactive and incorporate video elements. Don't sell -- tell stories that help your audience to see themselves in the message.

Speak to Influence

Tip #41

Stories Sell

Tell stories that relate to your product or service.

Tie the story in so that the prospect can see them in the story. Tell personal stories of how you overcame some of the same problems and the pain it caused in the process that they may have and how your product or service solved the problem.

Use your story to paint a picture of how your solution makes a difference in their lives. People love stories!

Be sure to incorporate stories in your sales process.

SPEAK TO INFLUENCE

TIP #42

UTILIZE TESTIMONIALS

Written and video testimonials are a powerful way to hear what a third party says about you, and your product or service. Someone else saying how great you are is better than YOU saying how great you are.

Get testimonials from clients who are similar to your prospects and work them into your sales presentation.

Oh yea, share your testimonials on social media too. It's a powerful way to get your client's into action.

Additional Tip: GIVE Testimonials FIRST. When you become known for giving testimonials, the recipients are more likely to send you one!

Speak to Influence

Tip #43

Weave and Seed

Weaving is a technique used by speakers to move their prospects to action. A good weave is strategically placed into your signature talk at a place where clients have an emotional reaction to your subject.

For instance, weave in a testimonial after a common pain point is presented. Ensure the testimonial addresses the pain point and how your product or service solved that point.

Speak to Influence

Tip #44

Educate

Don't use your speaking opportunity as a big sales pitch. Use it to educate your audience.

Through your presentation they will recognize themselves and identify the need for your product or service. Through stories or descriptive case studies share the lessons learned, the 3 steps, highlight this with language like "What I wish someone had shared with me sooner…"

With research into your audience and their needs, you can ensure they identify themselves in the story and are eager to purchase as a result.

Get good at educating and your audience will accept your call to action.

Speak to Influence

Tip #45

Blah, Blah, Blah

Don't be a boring talking head!

Speaking is an art that is learned. If you are not good at it, get some help. We have all heard the speaker who goes on and on and on. Break up the speech by being highly visual. If you can do a product or service demonstration, do so.

Be interactive and get the audience involved. Call people by name. Insert their names into your stories. There are many techniques that can be used to give an interesting, energetic speech. If you talk too much, your audience will be bored and worse yet, they won't buy.

Speak to Influence

Tip #46

Where to Speak

Identify speaking opportunities where you have a target market. Do some research online and find the associations that work with your target market. Contact those groups to find out if they need a speaker.

Visit the local chapter of that group or attend at the state or national level first and establish a relationship with the organizers.

Ask people who have seen you speak locally if they belong to any of those associations and ask them to recommend you as a speaker.

Speak to Influence

Tip #47

Give Something Away

When you speak, make sure you have a way to grow your email list. There's a couple of ways to build a giveaway into your presentation.

You could

1) have a drawing where you collect business cards (be sure to have slips of paper that your audience can fill out in case they don't have business cards)
2) you could have a digital giveaway like a white paper, ebook, checklist or video training where the audience signs up for your list and automatically receives your giveaway item.

Regardless of the method, the point is to get people to join your list so that you can capture them for your email list.

Speak to Influence

Tip #48

Practice, Practice, Practice

The key to being a great speaker is to practice.
The key to get past nervousness is to practice.
The key to getting clients to see you as
the expert in your field is to practice.

Repetitive practice makes for a polished delivery.
What is essential is to get started.

Try on your speech in front of a small audience, see what works and what doesn't, tweak and repeat. You will find that once you get your message down, and you get into a rhythm, your audience will want to do business with you because you are in the front of the room as the expert.

Technology Tools

Tip #49

Get Organized

One of the most effective technology tools for you to use is "Customer Relationship Management" (CRM) software.

With this software you'll increase your tracking abilities and be more organized in your follow up.

Is there a cost? Usually
Is there a learning curve? Yes.
Will it save you time in the long run? Absolutely.

Technology Tools
Tip #50

Use Social Media

Use social media to stay connected.

Whether you meet someone at a networking event or they are a participant in your audience, make sure you connect with them on social media. When networking, ask your new acquaintance what is their favorite social media platform.

If you can connect with them on your mobile device right then and there, do it. Mention any mutual connections that you share. This helps to break the ice and there is an instant connection. Doing this helps them to remember you and you can immediately start liking, commenting, and sharing their posts, which helps to solidify the relationship.

Technology Tools

Tip #51

Email Marketing ROCKS!

Email marketing is often overlooked as a way to stay connected to your connections. Email marketing is your way to remind people that you are in business and that you are there to serve them when they are ready.

Email is a tool that helps you to show up (often right when your prospect or client needs you). While social media is a great way to stay connected, the owners of the social media platform are in control of who you actually engage with.

With email, you get to show up in 100% of your followers' Inboxes and do a pageant wave to remind them you are still in business.

Technology Tools
Tip #52

What is a #Hashtag?

A hashtag is a great way to bring everyone together who are attending the same event, are following the same product or service or who are like minded.

Many movements were started with a simple #. For instance, when you are speaking, have your audience tweet or post your quotes with a designated hashtag that is branded to you.

Toni's Hashtag is #DrasticSteps
Elizabeth's Hashtag is #Soar2Success

Think of a hashtag as a file folder in a file cabinet- it organizes all the posts with the same hashtag together.

Technology Tools

Tip #53

There's an App for That!

There are many tech tools that are easily accessible on your phone to help you be more productive, network, market yourself, etc. Many of these tools are free or low cost and readily available.

Ask your friends what tools they use to stay on track and productive.

Let technology be your friend and make life easier for you.

Download a list of Favorite Apps at:
Soar2Success.com/Favorite-Apps

Technology Tools

Tip #54

Facebook

Facebook is a great networking tool to stay connected to those you meet in person. Stay connected to your prospects, clients, and networking friends by asking them if you can connect with them on social media. Once you are connected, start engaging with the person: "Like" their posts, comment on their posts positively and share.

This helps to develop a relationship with you because every time you engage with them they see your name and photo. This helps them to remember you when it's time to repeat business or when you need to contact them.

Social media is a powerful way to stay connected and keep them coming back for more of what you have to offer.

Technology Tools
Tip #55

Facebook (Yes- There's More)

Participate in a group, or better yet, start your own group.

Groups are a great way to gather your tribe. You can have discussions around your speeches, product or service.

A group is a great way to bring like-minded people together and connect them to one another. By having this interaction, your tribe shares ideas and gets to know one another and they see you as a people connector and want to engage with you fully.

Technology Tools

Tip #56

LinkedIn

LinkedIn is a great place to network when you are in a business community. If you are selling business to business, LinkedIn is the place to be. The power of LinkedIn is that it shows you the 6 degrees of separation from your key contact. So if you want to connect with the CEO of ABC Company, you can see how many of your connections are connected directly to him and you can ask for an introduction.

Introductions are a great door opener that often allows you to get in where a gatekeeper would normally keep you out.

Make a concentrated effort to engage with key people and it will turn into real business.

Technology Tools

Tip #57

Twitter

Twitter is a fast moving social media platform that allows people to post quick thoughts about an idea surrounding their service or product. The real power in Twitter is the use of #hashtag (See Tip #52).

Then there is the following. When someone follows you, follow back. Follow the followers of those who are ideal clients to you, attend the same events as you, and are in the niche you service.

And of course, the "retweet" where you share someone else's tweet to your following.

Follow Toni at @ToniHarrisSpeak
Follow Elizabeth at @PilotSpeaker

Technology Tools
Tip #58

Video

Video is magic!

Showcase your product or service in video. Create a 30-second commercial using video. You can talk about your product on your smartphone or tablet and share it on YouTube and your social medias.

Better yet, you can have your customers talk about your product and give you a testimonial that can be shared. This will help people to have confidence in you and your service.

By the way, imperfect videos ROCK! They are more authentic and trustworthy than a "perfect" video.

Don't worry about perfection -- it's not necessary.

Invest in Yourself

Tip #59

You CAN Invest in You

Investing time and money in you is good.

So many times we don't invest in ourselves because we are so busy or we feel we don't have the energy to put into additional certifications, degrees or education.

You have permission to invest in yourself NOW!

How can you expect anyone else to invest in YOU if you don't invest in YOU?

Start TODAY to grow and increase your expertise. Investing in you says, "I matter." In addition, you increase your confidence, which translates to more money and sales.

Invest in Yourself

Tip #60

Get Certified

Does a get certification matter?

It depends on your work and your area of expertise.

In financial services, getting certifications denote that you have put in the work to know your craft and to expand your expertise. A certification gives you the knowledge and tools to be able to be a better advisor for your clients and helps to instill confidence in you.

So yes, get certified, not only for your clients but also more importantly for yourself.

Invest in Yourself

Tip #61

Go Back To School

Do you want to get a degree? A degree is a great way to boost your confidence and skillset.

When Toni was in financial sales she didn't have a degree and was very successful, but when she found herself out of work and looking for a six-figure job, many doors were slammed shut! In 2009, Toni decided to take a drastic step and enroll in college. She did not want the lack of a degree to ever be a showstopper again. Now Toni has a Bachelor's and a Master's degree and the confidence in myself that goes with it.

Now there are so many online degree programs that are flexible in scheduling. It's never too late to go back to school.

Invest in Yourself

Tip #62

Look Good

Invest in your personal self.

When you are in sales, your potential customers judge you in the first 10 seconds of meeting you.

Make sure you look appropriate for your industry.

If you need a new wardrobe invest in a business wardrobe, if you need new style, invest in an image consultant or stylist.

A new look helps to boost your confidence and helps you to feel like you can take on any obstacle.

Make sure your image positively influences the sale and says, "Buy me!"

Invest in Yourself

Tip #63

Pay for Help

Got help?

If not, perhaps you should invest in getting help in your business. Smart business and sales people surround themselves with people who do the administrative tasks or the tasks that they simply are not good at.

It may be a drastic step to find and train help but it is well worth it to free your time to do what you do best, SELL!

Invest in Yourself

Tip #64

Hire a Coach

The best athletes and business people invest in a coach.

A coach can help you to see what's missing in your business and hold you accountable to your tasks.

A coach can help you to grow your business and share resources to help improve your efficiency and productivity.

A coach helps you to get out of your own way. If Kobe Bryant, Michael Jordan, Oprah Winfrey, Bill Gates, Steve Jobs and others all have coaches then why don't you think you need one?

Invest in Yourself

Tip #65

Be Intentional

Be intentional about growing in your knowledge.

Make a concentrated effort to read, listen to audios, watch videos, etc. Download audios to your smartphone and listen as you work. Find podcasts that educate and listen to those. Find a business, sales, or motivational book and read a little everyday.

Whatever the learning method you choose to use.
Be intentional about getting education in every day.

Those small investments in yourself can pay off greatly!

Invest in Yourself

Tip #66

Take a Seminar or Workshop

Learning does not have to be a long, drawn out process.

Take a workshop intensive to improve your skills.

If you need to sharpen your sales skills there are short workshops that can give you great tips to help improve your sales skills. Workshops can be from a half-day to a couple of days. They are a great way to invest in yourself because they are typically not expensive and you can get a lot of information in a short period of time.

Check out courses in your area and get signed up today!

Invest in Yourself

Tip #67

Take Care of Your Health

No health, no wealth.

If you don't invest in your health then you don't have a business. Invest time, money and energy into your health.

If you are not healthy, you cannot produce to the best of your ability. Do whatever it takes to get and stay healthy. Never be too busy to go to the doctor or participate in a workout activity.

Being in sales can be stressful, do what you need to do to make sure you take care of yourself first!

Invest in Yourself

Tip #68

Reward Yourself

Give yourself a prize for a win! Treat yourself to something nice. Go ahead, you earned it. The nice thing about sales is when you get big commissions you can do something fun with it.

Celebrate the wins of any size, large or small.

The next time you win a deal, REWARD yourself!

Closing Techniques

Tip #69

Ask for the Sale

Asking for the sale is a drastic step.

Remember that your prospect will be better off if they do business with you. Have the confidence to tell them that fact without being arrogant.

Know that the prospect just wants to know that their purchase with you won't hurt them. Assure them that you have their best interest at heart, then take the step and simply ask.

"What will it take to close this deal?"

The prospect might just say yes!

Closing Techniques

Tip #70

Close When the Client is Ready

If the client is jumping up and down with excitement, then guess what? It's time to close!

Sometimes our clients are giving us all kinds of buying signs and we ignore them; we have to make one more point, get out the entire presentation, or just keep talking until we talk the client right out of the sale.

When the client shows that they are ready, take that time to say, "let's do this!"

Shut up and close the deal!

Closing Techniques

Tip #71

Watch the Body Language

There are some clear body language signals that the client is ready to buy.

When the client leans in, they may be ready to buy. When the client does a little jig, they may be ready to buy. When the client opens up their body by uncrossing their arms or legs that is a signal that they may be ready to buy.

That may be a good time to ask clarifying questions and to ask for the sale.

Watch the body language; it can tell you a lot more than their mouth will.

Closing Techniques
Tip #72

Be Excited!

Are you excited about what you sell?

Then act like it!

Have you seen sales people who show no enthusiasm about their service or product? If you can't get excited about what you are offering, how can you expect anyone else to?

If you want your client to buy, let your enthusiasm show on the outside.

There is a word of caution here. Don't be so enthusiastic that it appears fake or that your prospect gets weirded out by you. Over-enthusiasm can backfire, so make sure it's authentic!

Closing Techniques

Tip #73

Uncover The Pain

Understand the pain that your product solves for your client and be sure to address this SPECIFICALLY during the sales presentation.

People typically buy for two reasons
1. to relieve the pain or
2. to experience pleasure.

If your product or service addresses their pain then you are likely to be able to close the sale.

Ask enough questions to get to the root of their problem and repeat back to them how your service will solve that problem.

Closing Techniques
Tip #74

Ask Questions

The close question is one that gets them to answer, "yes" to the question of whether they understand what you are offering and can they see how the benefits of your product can help them in their lives, business, etc.

Mention their pain point again and ask,

"Based on our conversation, do you think that my product can serve you and take away some of your pain?"

If they answer yes, ask for the close.

If they answer no or they are not sure, ask them to share why not so you can clear up any objections.

Closing Techniques

Tip #75

Listen

God gave us two ears and one mouth for a reason!

A good salesperson listens carefully and talks less.

Let the prospect talk. Listen for clues for pain points. Don't be so eager to jump in.

Ask questions, let them talk.
Often times your prospect will talk themselves into your product. Take notes and pay attention.

Mirror their body language and repeat what you heard for clarification.

Closing Techniques

Tip #76

Make It An Easy Yes!

Offer your prospect choices.

Give them low, mid and high level choices.
Most people go for the middle.

When given options, people will typically make a choice.

It's hard to say no to multiple items.

Make your clients an easy yes offer that's irresistible.

Closing Techniques
Tip #77

Offer Bonuses

Remember the saying, "You get what you pay for," now the saying is "you get more than what you pay for."

People like to think they are getting something for nothing, so offer bonuses to the sale.

A bonus could be a book, a companion product, additional training, or a VIP service.

There are many things that can be a value added bonus.

You can also partner with other people in your network to add additional bonus tools that promotes them into your client base. Give people more than what they pay for and they will keep coming back for more!

Closing Techniques

Tip #78

Take Away The Fear

People hesitate to buy from fear of making a mistake.

Have you ever bought something and someone questioned, "Why did you buy that?"

How did that make you feel? Well, your client has the same fear. People want to look smart for the decisions they make. They want to be proud that they got a great value or that your product or service will improve their life.

Make sure you take the sting of making the wrong decision away from the buyer and it will be easier for them to say, "Yes!"

Other Titles in the Soar 2 Success Series

Find More Online at
Soar2SuccessBooks.com

Other Titles in the Soar 2 Success Series

Find More Online at
Soar2SuccessBooks.com

Other Titles in the Soar 2 Success Series

Find More Online at
Soar2SuccessBooks.com

Other Titles in the Soar 2 Success Series

Find More Online at
Soar2SuccessBooks.com

A Note from Toni

I hope you found this book easy to read and were able to implement a few tips in your sales and marketing strategies.

Pick a few and concentrate on those. Add a few more every week and pretty soon you will see drastic results in your sales and business.

These strategies have worked for me and I know they will work for you too.

The key is to be focused and committed, and pretty soon it won't be drastic it your business will be fantastic!

Toni

About Toni Harris

Award winning, five star rated speaker and marketing strategist, Toni Harris is a expert at helping her clients achieve drastic results! With over 25 years experience as an entrepreneur, including 14 years as a financial advisor and manager, Toni's unique strategies help her clients to thrive!

Toni's proven strategies helps her clients transition from a salary mindset to an entrepreneurial mindset and increase their revenue exponentially. One of Toni's clients went from a $28K salary to over $150K in commission! Toni Harris walks the talk and is currently the #1 sales rep in North America for Constant Contact.

Are you ready to take your business to a higher level? If so, hire Toni Harris to educate, motivate, and transform your audience to breakthrough their barriers and achieve drastic results today!

Book Toni for your next meeting or training event:

info@ToniHarris.com
ToniHarris.com

Connect On Social Media at:

facebook.com/drasticsteps
twitter.com/toniharrisspeak
linkedin.com/in/toniharrisspeak
youtube.com/toniharrisspeak

About Elizabeth McCormick

Elizabeth shattered the glass ceiling in the military as an Army Black Hawk Pilot, then in her corporate career as a global contract negotiator. And now she continues to rain glass as an in demand International Motivational Speaker and CEO of Soar 2 Success International.

As a decorated U.S. Army Black Hawk Helicopter Pilot, Elizabeth flew missions such as Air Assault/Rappelling, Command & Control, VIP, and Military intelligence. She supported United Nations peacekeeping operations in Kosovo, receiving the Meritorious Service Medal for her excellence in service, and in 2011 Elizabeth was awarded the Congressional Veteran Commendation.

Elizabeth is a founding member of the John Maxwell Team of speakers, coaches and trainers, and a dynamic energizing entertainer inspiring audiences worldwide.

More About Elizabeth McCormick

A frequent face in the media, Elizabeth has been seen on ABC, CBS, FOX News, MSNBC, in the Wall Street Journal and more. A No. 1 best-selling author, her personal development book, *The P.I.L.O.T. Method*, is a "must read"!

Text **SOAR to 96000** to receive free training videos.

Book Elizabeth to Speak at Your Next Event:

PilotSpeaker.com
BlackHawk@PilotSpeaker.com
Linkedin.com/in/PilotSpeaker
Twitter.com/PilotSpeaker
Facebook.com/BlackHawkPilot

About Soar 2 Success International

Founded in 2012, Soar 2 Success International has rapidly grown to be a premier speaking and training company representing high quality professional speakers. Soar 2 Success added a Publishing division in 2013 and already has more than 20 titles in process.

Find Speakers, Books and Publishing information at:

Soar2Success.com

Connect with us at:

Facebook.com/soar2success

Twitter.com/soar2successint